Selected Poems

CHRIS MCCULLY was born in Bradford, Yorkshire in 1958 and now lives and works in the Netherlands, where he writes poems, textbooks and works on fly-fishing and gives freelance courses on aspects of using the English language. For many years he taught at the University of Manchester, and he remains chairman and co-director of the Modern Literary Archives programme at the John Rylands University Library in Manchester. Chris McCully travels widely, making up to a dozen overseas trips a year in order to write features for the fly-fishing press in the UK and Netherlands. His recent work includes his poetry collection *Polder* (Carcanet), *The Sound Structure of English* (Cambridge University Press) and *Fishing and Pike Lures* (Medlar Press), all published in 2009, with further projects in preparation such as *Outside*, a book of essays on natural history and the northern Netherlands (Two Ravens Press, 2011), a travel book, *From the Last Sane Places on Earth* (Carcanet, 2013) and a co-authored book on Irish sea-trout and sea-trout fishing *(Irish Sea-trout: Nomads of the Tides* (Medlar Press).

Also by Chris McCully from Carcanet Press

Poetry
Time Signatures
Not Only I
The Country of Perhaps
Polder

Prose
The Poet's Voice and Craft

Translation
Old English Poems and Riddles

CHRIS McCULLY

Selected Poems

CARCANET

First published in Great Britain in 2011 by
Carcanet Press Limited
Alliance House
Cross Street
Manchester M2 7AQ

A CIP catalogue record for this book is available from the British Library

ISBN 978 1 84777 018 9

The publisher acknowledges financial assistance from Arts Council England

Typeset by XL Publishing Services, Tiverton
Printed and bound in England by SRP Ltd, Exeter

For my family

Acknowledgements

Fleur Adcock, Agada Ammeraal, Joy Anderson, Andy Bell, Brian Cox, Valerio Cugia, Steve Glosecki, Stella Halkyard, Martin Harrison, Chris Jones, Marjoke Kuipers, Grevel Lindop, Helen Maclean, Rosie Paice, Rob Rollison, Kevin Rutherford, Copland Smith, Gavin Smith, Fraser Steele, Anne Stevenson, Mary Syner, Margaret Whittle, Carol Willis, Fergus Wilde – these friends, teachers and former colleagues commented critically and constructively on some of the drafts of some of the poems in this volume. Monika, Tess and the family have my love. I am most grateful to you all, and as always, I am particularly grateful to Michael Schmidt and to my very fine editor at Carcanet Press, Judith Willson. Without Michael's continuing interest and support, and without Judith's kind and acute reading of my work, I doubt I would have continued to publish any verse whatsoever. Thank you.

Contents

Preface

It's a curious experience, selecting one's own poems for publication. On what grounds should one select? Chronological? Thematic? The poems which seem to go over best in readings or the poems about which one receives the most correspondence? The poems which gave one most technical difficulty or those which are, to the selector, the most personally meaningful?

It was a puzzle, and made the more difficult because I'd never expected to be in a position to produce such a work. Hardy, Yeats, Graves and Auden – these were the poets I most associated with 'Selected Poems'. As a young man I re-read those volumes so often that they sometimes fell apart. Volumes by Pound, Stevens and Lowell followed them into partial or complete disintegration. I never expected to be asked to produce such a work myself. I'm still astonished that I was so asked.

In terms of my own work, there were some longer poems, such as the quasi-fugal 'Mass' which appeared in *The Country of Perhaps* (2003), which I didn't think suitable for selection (certainly not in their entirety) on the grounds of length. A book such as this, I reasoned, should offer a representative and accessible selection of the writer's work, and 'Mass' wasn't truly representative. On the other hand, there were some medium-length translations from Old English (the poem known as 'The Seafarer' is an example, whose translation I was working on during 2006–8) whose structure and themes might be judged 'inaccessible' by some present-day readers but which nevertheless have very deep technical and thematic links with some of the writing I was doing thirty years ago, and which I engage with still. Some of these medium-length translations are, therefore, represented here.

I doubted, too, whether to include the parallelistic prose-poem 'Dust', which appeared at the beginning of *Polder* (2009) though it had been drafted and re-drafted many years before (1998–2004). One kind reviewer, however, pointed out that the resonances of what is a pretty bleak exploration of mortality were sufficiently strong to allow the shorter lyric poems placed after it in the collection to read as a response to the intricate nihilism of 'Dust'. That was precisely one intention of *Polder*: to allow civility, good manners, memories of friendship and collegiality to reply to the nothings that may come of nothing, and to insist accordingly on the teeming reality of what may be imaginatively constructed out of dust, even if that turns out to be merely a beautiful desolation. Therefore in these selected poems I also and eventually chose to include 'Dust', and again placed it at the beginning of the collection so that the poems which succeed the piece may be read as fragments of consolation, of partial vision, of a tempered, amended voice.

With shorter lyrics I compromised. I selected one poem ('The Flood and the Tree') written while I was still an undergraduate in Newcastle-upon-Tyne, and one ('The Vinegar Days', the last piece in this volume) written when I was fifty. I included poems which readers and listeners have told me they enjoyed, together with some of those poems about which I received wonderfully kind and constructive, if infrequent, letters. I also selected one or two poems which won some sort of runner-up prize, such as 'An Auction for Amsterdam' and 'Fishermen on Santa Monica Pier', although I confess that the prize-winning, encouraging though it was, was of less importance than the fact that the poems are as adept, appropriate and sparing as I could have made them. Finally, I selected poems which, while not perhaps immediately popular, nevertheless embody some of my formal preoccupations, as these have manifested themselves over what are now many years. That is, it seemed important to include, alongside the many poems constructed in non-metrical verse, a range of metrical work – different kinds of sonnets, villanelles, ballad stanzas and so on. In a gesture which I hope will please the open-minded, there's one poem which aspires to the graphic ('for clive /s/cott'); in a gesture which I hope will please the curious, there's one pantoun ('The Gravy People'). Perhaps I should add that I have never consciously sat down to write a poem in such-and-such a form. The alignment of any poem with its eventual metre is a matter of listening and reading, patience and silence. Surrounded by that silence, I have over the years abandoned far more work than I have ever felt easy about committing to print, so in choosing the work for this volume I was selecting from what was already a selection.

I chose pieces which I hoped were varied, attractive and precise – 'the best words, in the best order'. It didn't seem possible to get beyond Coleridge's homely definition.

Chris McCully

Textual Note

In preparing this work, I've occasionally adjusted the original punctuation and have corrected some minor errors. In one poem, 'From the Country of Perhaps', I deleted a block of text which wasn't earning its keep. I've also adjusted the typography of some metrical poems so as to ensure that the beginning of each line is capitalised, and have generally used British customs of hyphenation in compound words composed of two free morphemes, preferring, for example, 'sign-post' to 'signpost'.

The translations from Old English confronted me with a further problem. The originals are written on vellum (calf-skin) and run margin-to-margin. I originally set the half-lines so that each rightmost half-line had a justified leftmost edge. I did so to make the aural architecture of such verse graphically clear. That is, in the translations which appeared in *Old English Poems and Riddles* (2008), one encounters lines set on the page as follows:

> It's as though a kind of gift   had been given to my people.
> If he comes vicious,   it's him they'll want to capture.

Though Grevel Lindop had warned me that such a graphic arrangement might be construed as a tacit invitation to read the resultant columns of half-lines vertically (so that in the above, 'If he comes vicious' would be read immediately after, and subordinate to, 'a kind of gift'), I'm afraid I didn't heed his warning: I couldn't believe that anyone would be so ignorant of the originals, or of the many modern editions of Old English poems, so to read, or to wish to read. Nevertheless, two or three critics attempted such columnar readings, and thereafter complained that the result made no sense. Of course it didn't: neither the original poems nor their translations were constructed in that way. To discourage any such misreading, I've here set the lines so that four spaces exist between the two half-lines which comprise each line:

> It's as though a kind of gift   had been given to my people.
> If he comes vicious,   it's him they'll want to capture.

Such a graphic arrangement will be more than familiar to anyone who has studied any modern edition of an Old English, Old Saxon, Old High German or Eddic poem, where one's eye becomes very accustomed to (in the words of one of my more trenchant, metaphorical and grumbly critics) 'leaping the gutter'.

Apart from those minor tweakings, the texts of the poems are almost exactly the same as those found in those previous volumes of mine which Carcanet have been generous enough to publish.

The solutions to the riddles, incidentally are as follows: p. 75, fish in the river; p. 79, wine.

from *Polder*
(2009)

Dust

I have looked into dust.

Dust is in the Bechstein, the dahlias are dust, the stray horse under its clouded moon is dust. All the somewheres where everyone once was combed the future for someone in particular and found nothing but dust. The elderly schoolmasters and piano-teachers are dust, and the leaves of the piano primer were eaten, note by note, by dust. Dust is in the Venice piazzas, and the bed full of sunlight is dying of drifted skin that has already become dust. There was dust in the air under the airplane wing, dust under the thumbtack, dust in the fingernail. The exercise books and student notes aim towards dust until they burst in a cloud of smoke, a censer and a thwarted hosanna, where dust covers the choir-stall, and the cope of farewell.

Age shall not wither her, nor shall it weary them, whoever she was and whoever they are, but age was already in the first thought of weariness, because there was dust – dust in the billet, dust at the cenotaph, dust in the greenroom, dust in the hymn-book, dust in the piano-stool and the abandoned ashtray.

As I say, I have looked into dust.

★ ★ ★ ★

There are others who will speak to you about the sea, the sea. Not I. Others will write to you about the loss that everyone was and the griefs that are in every change of key. Not me. There are even the distinguished voices of the agonised that will show you fear in a handful of dust, but that isn't the dust I mean, beloved. And there are those from the future who will, with a calm sneer, inform you tomorrow that everything becomes the night. But that's not right.

I'll tell you about dust.

You have the memories. You have the Insta-Snaps in bundles, the framed photographs of weddings propped on the television. You have the television. You have the presents of the lost faces, the travelling rug from Istanbul, the blue Greek carpet in the bathroom, the unframed icon made by an Albanian itinerant, the occasional table gifted to you by a one-legged carpenter whose life was already over. You have the radio that someone bought you six birthdays ago. Yes, you think you have memories – the indiscreet peelings of underwear, the mouth whose tongue erected you from the lees of the Burgundy; you have the letters of the mouth bundled in a whisky crate at the back of the closet. And you can't bear to open the whisky, the letters, the memories. This is because you haven't inherited memories. You have inherited... Dust? No. It isn't yet quite dust. You have inherited childhoods, all of them yours.

★ ★ ★ ★

'Childhood?' you'll say, not appearing to welcome this tacit invitation to think about yourself. 'But I'm not my childhood. Well, I'm not... I'm hardly... a child. I may retain parts of the child I was once but...'

You're thinking about this the wrong way.

Childhood is not the endless recitation of the past, where the past repeats itself by rote and rhythm like a Latin declension until eventually the voice falters at exactly the place where the fist was raised, and insistent fingers shook tomorrow by its throat. *Amo, amas, amat*; *mensa, mensa, mensam*; *dominus, domine, dominum*. Doh–re–mi. The first true note just happens to be *amo*.

But as you point out, you have changed. The language isn't the same, the declensions has lost their inflections and the rhythm has run into the hiatus of its own failures.

Elsewhere, someone is practising scales.

I don't want to invoke the shibboleths of the analyst's couch – can't you see the dust falling through the sunlight as the sunlight opens like mother in the eyes of the heavy brocade curtains? I'm not summoning the demons of betrayal, the poisons of untruth and distance, the reasons for an altered life.

You have changed. You've shed many skins. Your previous imago is an endless set of shucks. I wonder if you've ever wondered where the skins go? No? Not onto the fencepost like the leavings of a giant insect that has outgrown the nutrients of its incipient life? Not into the nugatory shards in the wasteland? No? No fragments, not even a nail-paring, to shore against your ruin? No?

No – the tacit No that began when childhoods became dust. It became the reason why you find it difficult to remember the face of the name where all the accusations had to begin. Dust glazed the photograph. The inner raptus of memory began to peel away in sunburn. Face it: the leavings were all over the house. Where did all the dust come from – the dust under the piano, the smear on the skirting-board, the grey glaze under the bathroom mirror, the tufts of drift under the bed?

It's skin.

It is technically only skin, the set of all the days of skin you have outgrown and will keep outgrowing beyond, beloved, the day you are no longer conscious of skin. Where did you think the nail-parings went? Where the hard skin and the verruca, the treated wart? Where the snuff-dry hay in the stable and the blasted rose? Where the scurf in the curry-comb? And the withered dahlias? And the black spray of so many questions?

D'you love me	*Dust*
Do you still love me	*Dust*
Is it all right	*Dust*
Who was she	*Dust*
Will it ever be	*Dust*
Is there a future	*Dust*
Will you ever	
Do you remember	*Dust*
Your lover	*Dust*
Do you still love me	

It will always be dust.

★ ★ ★ ★

Where do the days begin? The unreal slaver of the poet's sea? What does a look at the moon encounter? Where does the dandruff come from? The ash in the wind? Where does the bonfire go?

Where do you think the dust in the house called Sorry came from? A casual exhaust fume? The passing remnants of clouds speeding summer as it passed? The scab in the armpit of a gondolier? It came from you, and the cycle of shedding solitudes.

You became without your solitude, and left dust.

★ ★ ★ ★

We're thick with it, under the airplane wing, under the penumbra of Los Angeles smog, on the lamps in the brothels of Piraeus and

Delhi. Dust in the streetlamps; dust in the snow. Whirled with violence round about the pendant world, like a muff of gravity. Where does it all come from? Where everyone must go.

But who knows where dust began, and where the epic of drift will end? What first mote was in whose first eye, where was somewhere, and when was somewhere anywhere?

★ ★ ★ ★

I have looked into dust.

The first mote was beyond space or time. It was a word but it was beyond a word. It was an infinite point of density in No-time, in the beginning before the beginning was. It wasn't even yet a thought.

And there in the first mote was the first dust of all the worlds that had been before No-time — dust of castles, of extinct elephants, of the remaining snuff of eminent literary editors, of the nuclear fume from distant suns, of pumice stones and ejected pomegranate seeds, of popes, pan-scrubs, bank-managers, billets, the dispersed lava of a million volcanoes, of the dried tears of maimed marriages, relics of another explosion. It was the billionth shard, the ten trillionth husk. It was the catch in the throat that comes just before the childhood of the lover's heartbreaking, perennial cry: Be what I want, not what you need.

Be what I want, not what you need.

It's the cry in the faces of the wedding photographs that stare back at you from their unanointed places on top of the television. Dust blinds the stares.

But the cry doesn't know itself as a cry. Perhaps it never did, and had merely gathered into an infinitely dense, infinitely heavy point composed of all the cries of all the lovers of the worlds. It had collapsed into dust, and endlessly collapsing, became a mote.

Gravity, beloved. It was all collapsing, like the weight in the air of a lung. Something was breathing. Dust was the breath of the gods.

And in the breath, a mote. In the beginning, before the beginning was, since there could be no beginning since whatever was breathing couldn't be conscious of a beginning. Where does a breath begin and end? With the remnant of the last pulmonary stroke? Or the beginning of the next?

And there was the mote of the worlds.

18

★ ★ ★ ★

Out it all came, accelerating into solitudes and disconsolation, and all the somewheres that were still to be. Out came the rivers, the birds' nests, the stories; out came the cutlery and the manicure sets; out came the tired children and the exhausted lovers, not knowing whose was which. Out came the elephants and iguanas; out came the alcoholics and the bishops; out came the doers of good works and those who simply wanted a cigarette; out came the arks and the doctors; out came Venice; out came Michaelangelo and Milton, each looking surprised. Out came Beethoven, seeming furious. Out came the mothers and the analysts, the accusations and the prophets; out came the suicides and the wedding photographs; the in-trays and the dead letter drops; out came people called Cheryl and Steve, Emma and Anthony, Wolfgang and Anastasia, and two sisters looking for a wild horse. Out came the grey smear of dawn over city skylines, and a nest of spiders. Out came the blood of a summer afternoon. Out came the Latin declensions. Out dropped a clouded moon; out came the Goldberg Variations and the airline attendants; out came a Bechstein; out came a piano stool and a pair of arthritic hands. Out came a boy; out came a bed with bloodstained sheets, and lovers' letters. Out came the goodbyes and all the voices of all the children that would be dust in the house called Sorry.

A later age than this will inspect the disaster through telescopes and infra-red imaging, and call it a brief history of time.

★ ★ ★ ★

And out came the voice that is this, now, from the universal explosion, whose background radiation you can still hear in the dial of the radio and still see in the afterglow of the switched-off television. And that voice too will be dust, and dust again the voices of the pages and the voices of the lovers.

For a while it will hold together. Gravity, beloved. History is heavy with dust. But something is breathing, always beyond consciousness or witness, and in time, through times beyond witness, the dust will begin to gather, and lie again in the dahlias and the cricket pavilions, and settle in the air of sunlit afternoons in Berlin; and the Venetian piazzas will slowly sink under its weight, century after century, where not even this voice – which is yours, beloved – will be waiting, since the waiting will have become the movement of dust; and the voices and the radios, the air-conditioners, the aspirations, the minor odysseys of the broken heart will become for an instant, and then will have been, and will all have been dust.

★

from *Time Signatures*
(1993)

Bede's Copyist

I have no proper name, yet his is tall
On Europe's stones and in the candleflukes
Whose culture briefly held a sparrow's brawl
In a crowned head. We set it down in books,
A lettered Latin – that bird, this birth, that stall –
      With no mistakes.

Outside, the snow almost obscures the park,
Our wooden Christ's obliterated face.
Inside, with all the negligence of grace
His habit falls across my page's mark.
Again we work between space and space –
      And both are dark.

Houses

They seem solid: render and Accrington brick;
Good lines; set angles on a suburb slope
Where no one hears (the walls are two feet thick)
The neighbours loudly drinking down their hope.
But scaffolding's erected everywhere
And yesterday these houses' roofs were gone;
The day before, the stonework layer by layer
Vanished into dance-hall whistling and the sun.

Foundations turned to foot-prints, which grew back
To moor and coppiced hazel; road bled a spring
Where horses drank; and through the Zodiac
The past unravelled on its stick of string
Until what made the paid-for future there
Were merely geese and winter, sleet and air.

The Flood and the Tree

The winter flood took the one white tree
and the one white tree became part of the river,
uprooted and at rest, fields downstream.

It won't move now from its backwater.

Into the calm spring currents it puts out green.

Pastoral

Come to the years of tup and serve
loveless, the weaner crisping
on the heap, flies that carve
air into slices, dogs sleeping
beyond the boundaries in a yard of sun.

Walk with me with the axe and no one
up field edges, feeling the bit.
Tell me the white grub at the root,
the valves of sows, teat and snout,
the carcase – as if you had expected it.

Some Say

I wish I were the river. Its power now
in flood obliterates
everything it once thought about itself:
on the valley stones, on this winter floor among the rocks
it slides through its own skin like a brown snake.

Elsewhere, perhaps, it's become a lake
for migrating birds, snow-flakes or reflections of low cloud;
elsewhere, almost unimaginably, past pipes and drums,
the luxury of knotted towns and confluence, oil in the estuary
and wharves where ships no longer build,
it's become the sea –

turns blue in August, is mackerel-tide
or salt-secreting cell in the anemone's claw,
disperses until the salmon smell it out,
evaporates, is sun-smashed, hauls through the winds,
repeats itself in isobars and the blowing sky, is mist and cloudburst
for summer's same greens riddling on their boughs.

Some say the river's purpose is the sea;
others say – deftly casting a fly – its fish,
rising to sedge in the half-light or
spawning on redds in the uplands where no hand is.
Others see purpose in its geography,
its gathering of loose stuff from the hill-sides,
straw and branch and blood-stained fleece, the watershed
exacting its price. For others
it's the haunting of fossils. Others simply think
its purpose is dogs and exercise, their favourite walk.

But here, in time where springs evolve
obscurely from reed and blackened brick, the flood supposes
nothing of its animate purposes.
Watching this twisting, unslackening rope of water pass
towards whatever end, leaving its new course
printed on bent stem and flattened, silver grass...

The river is the eye that looks at it.

'Toward the unknown region'

Wry light on slate,
leaving the darkening trees.
How up at Oughtershaw the sky comes in
to roofs and branches, a dog,
a locked pub,
and martins under the eaves.

And the river, the river
below, its fish exciting the pools,
the water-grain perceptible as night comes on
to roofs and branches, a van,
a sign-post north,
and lately a moving bird.

It is the stranger wanting peace
at the watershed knows peace recedes
beyond each stride, finds nothing
but roofs and branches, placing
the salience of water and stone
and journeys behind him vanishing.

Swifts, Conistone Bridge

Always looked for; always late arriving –
and the air is there for their quick conniving:

they glance at water and the summer's rind
whose temperature is insects and the green tundra
growing monochrome for moth and spinner,
the fly-fisher on his failing reach
come night, come quietness, where resumes
their restlessness, fragility.

Luckily over the lucid river
skim these far and momentary travellers,
instinctively aiming, connecting
the brink of eye with eye: the slim
nerves of the evening's shutting sky.

The world slides into the dark on its slow rim.

Living in Greenfield

for Martin Harrison

Even in this black village full of weather
you can smell money: house-prices are rising
around Harold's bakery; Walter Cox, Cobbler,
stitches and rivets more expensive leather;
and track-suited incomers jog in headphones
            towards the tall finances
            of the rest of the century.

Already we've made a buck. The house next door
fetches so many K ('moorland on all sides –
close to bus-route – gas c.h. – much sought-after')
and tomorrow will be worth a few K more.
This paper money makes us easily pleased:
            we sit on our investment
            like a pair of hills.

And the phone rings. People come out to stay
because we're scenery. The edge of the map
curls up with Pennines and quaintness; easy walks
we never take; views; distances; the long affray
of high moor-lines haunting a Gothic novel.
            And things better left unmentioned:
            inbreeding; dead children; the mad.

I pack up my books and head towards the train
past Harold's shop and Walter Cox's shoes,
towards the city glowing in its durance
through the commuter dark of seven o'clock.
Still it's cold, and February – too cold for rain,
and even the morning joggers are in bed.
            The air, bitter, disastrous,
            Is stained with snow and bread.

In the Summer Train

Summer's this wilderness of weeds and shunting-yards,
earth-works of the iron claw, of rust in grass.
Someone's half-silenced radio hisses the Second Test.

Across the aisle, three women are playing cards.
The ticket-collector's eyeballs slyly pass
five virgins with their unlit cigarettes.

Everything's on the slide: a dusty swallow,
a paper on the floor, a hand in its own sweat,
a ripple of tattoos and greasy hair.

Heat simmers at diesel-oil and rosebay willow,
and smell's the only movement here: a vague meat –
perhaps a long-lost cat becoming air.

The slow train has stalled again at Miles Platting.
England are batting.

Finding a Fossil

This ammonite curled up in early stone
decreed it should become a paper-weight.
Through every date –
of cooling fern, glacier and trammelled bone,
growth-rings unspooling on unknown trees –
while the mammoth world grew ruinous
it became flood-water, upland, broached by sea;
lay turned, rain-struck, for anyone's keen eyes.

And found me.

Union Street

He met his true love on Union Street.
The clock filled with minutes, the night with hurry;
Time contracted to sorry and worry
And the sky was orange with city and sleet
When he met his true love on Union Street.

His true love's eyes were the holly thorn:
Winter had glossed their look with cold.
And he lay there waiting to be told
It would have been better if he'd never been born
Since his true love's eyes were the holly thorn.

His true love's mouth had his mother's lips,
Scrubbed with the Bible, wafers and bread.
She breathed him close, and he cradled his head,
Holding her voice in his black finger-tips:
His true love's mouth had his mother's lips.

His true love's reach was the frozen stone,
Pavements for parking and the busker's case,
The metals of spit and the stars' turned face
And the last church hour that struck alone
For his true love's reach and the frozen stone.

His true love left him on Union Street.
The parked cars were tangled in wind-scuffled trees;
Snow fell from stars like a childhood disease;
And the drunks at midnight said *'Scuse me pal please*
Until the bored sirens helped him to meet
His true love meet him on Union Street.

Rain

You should have seen the rain.
The hill was Lear's bald head left to the falling storm
and darkness shocked itself, in a springing wave buried the road,
the valley and the singing stones, and each house
went out completely, like a switched-off brain;
        and you should have seen the rain –
stotting down so hard it melted hair and washed away
fences, pylons, all landmarks; fused lights; broke roofs;
and stopped the diesels underground in floods
(the water rising, hands hammering each pane);
        but you should have seen the rain
that night, last night, the very last – the howling stacks,
the gutters full, and all the fish swept smoothly out to sea
and back again, dispersed among the sky-reflecting fields,
fields of white noise, the static hiss of rain on rain,
        the rain you should have seen,
the broken storm, endless, the storm with strength
to hurt itself, with strength to erase my name
and yours, whether we lay apart listening to the rain
or in each other's arms and felt the rain,
imagining the dark rain walking towards us, the bane
stored up for us from the beginning of might-have-been.
        You should have seen – it was almost marvellous –
        you should have seen the rain which cancelled us.

from *Not Only I*
(1996)

The Glass

A whisky eye
Reads back its age
Until the boy
It couldn't love
Has formed the page
And language of
Goodbye the boy
Mistook for joy,
Not only I.

Song

All summer's unsafe,
The north wind and leaf,
Its green turned like grief
On willow, white willow.

I walked through the places
I know that her face is,
Found just empty spaces
And willow, white willow.

She told me the danger
I turned into anger
And day made a stranger
Of willow, white willow.

What loved me that morning
Had failed by its evening;
What showed me the warning
Was willow, white willow.

Now what I must mean
Is north wind, leaf vein,
The summer worn down
To willow, white willow.

These eyes looking out
At what they must doubt
Find no heat or light
But willow, white willow –

No heart's ease, dry blood,
Ash turned in the wood,
Green vanishing for good
And willow, white willow.

Time Difference

Since you and I were spaced five hours apart
I checked your days against my watch all week –
Your solitary breakfasts my first drink,
Your evening book my last. And still my heart
Beat half a night ahead, too fast to think
Of anything but if things stayed the same:
If one was where the other couldn't look;
The Atlantic's separation of our name.

You moved within the life I'd left behind.
Elsewhere I talked, half blind, to any face,
Wanting the earth to move the dark to wind
Each hour-hand on our wrists to each right place.

In thirty thousand feet's returning blue
I saw sun rise at midnight. You came true.

Gold in the Hudson

Subtract the metal from the skin.
Don't mind that gold becomes the clay.
Walk down the wharf whose bridges burned
Nine hundred wedding nights away.

Finger's lighter by a circle
Whose years and diamond slipped their mark
But flesh still wears its round of bruises
Bent by pressure in the dark.

This river's full of marriages.
Don't stay to watch your wishing pitch
On oil and flotsam, floating lights:
Enough to know the river's rich.

Simply take...

...200lb of shadow
and a worried man.
Cut into average pieces
and sear over a naked flame
to seal in the juice.

Augment with middle age,
and season. Then

separately combine
a scant affair and overdraft
and set aside.

Add marriage to the meat,
with bouquet garni
of mortgages and pensions,
letters, photographs,
and wine to taste.

Allow to simmer,
checking from time to time
that the pan doesn't dry
(adding more wine and Epsom salts if so,
stirring continually).

Check seasoning, then fold in
divorce and impotence
(prepared earlier).

Remove from the pan,
and serve on a bed
of interesting courgettes,
decorating with some thinly-sliced guilt
at the last moment.

NB. Not suitable for home freezing.
Do not re-heat.

The Taxi

Whatever you think now don't let me know.
The taxi's waiting in your next affair;
It must be paid however far you go.

Someone will cash a cheque, and other hands grow
Familiar with your face as mine, or air.
Whatever you think now don't let me know.

Hurt's habits need new clothes, a portmanteau
Packed tight on tick and charged to anywhere.
It must be paid however far you go.

Load up the phones and memories. You owe
Them nothing that suggests you came to care.
Whatever you think now don't let me know.

Doors slam on half a life that seems to show
Goodbye can be as dear as it's unfair.
It must be paid however far you go.

Expensive exits, years of to and fro,
The meter running on your voice and stare:
Whatever you think now, don't let me know
It must be paid, however far you go.

Hiroshima

A thousand paper cranes define
new traffic   bird-song   people

that glitter of air and sound

and the shadow of a man
burnt into the ground

The Inscriptions

What she left, not took away
Touched me the more. Things can replace
With any cheque-book stub, delay
The shock of finding no known face.

Yet all that stayed involved our taste,
Together's plural choices: how
Undone and mine and run to waste –
The details hardly matter now.

And most, what had been given in
Auspicious moments, smiling looks
Whose wishes turned so peregrine:
All those inscriptions; all those books.

Scipio's Dream

He said he saw everything from a great height:
the water jug and cup, bulb in the bedside light.
He could hear even the smallest dust touching the floor.
It had all become impossibly, terribly clear.

Each afternoon he was wheeled to the window for air.
'What moves is angels, weight is love. The atmosphere
is flame, whose rings have stars for fire,' he wrote –
explaining himself away in his last known note.

Ave Atque Vale

Who hasn't, sitting in isolation,
　　Come to the belief
They aren't worth half their object, passion,
　　And are stiff with grief?

Lovers in unenviable apartments,
　　Knowing they're alone,
Hug their unseduced deportments,
　　Eye the telephone.

Medallion-men on well-paid beaches
　　Are invariably sad,
Keep for company three pet cockroaches
　　And a client who's mad.

Drunks, slow on busy boulevards,
　　Could easily be us,
Rambling for dollars in random words –
　　Love's point and terminus.

Hookers under lamplight crook
　　A knee becomingly,
But however lucrative the trick
　　The credit's temporary.

You're free. Everyone and no one bothers.
　　I sing a face from air.
Each shares with poets and their mothers
　　The culture of despair.

One always pays for conversation.
　　Another's charged for joy.
Beloved's just a passing fashion
　　Whose pattern buried Troy.

Think on. Don't answer. To the knock
    Where happiness occurs
Consider what can kill the luck
    Whose kiss and taste were hers.

I've learned not to reply. Although
    I realise that pain
Like worry tends to last, still I
    Won't say this much again.

from *The Country of Perhaps*
(2002)

Icarus

He was mad with it:
the intricacies of construction,
the wax that sealed each joint
to a workable point;
the local clarities of angles,
feathers; whatever could explain
the assemblage and harness it
to the dynamics of the sky.

He was mad with it,
and as the air glazed
without effort under the beating wings,
as the olive groves and the blue zoo
of the sea receded merely
to hillsides and ocean,
a disarticulated view,
he had succeeded.

He was mad with it –
the whole beautiful engineering.
But turning westwards, higher,
becoming pressure, becoming weight,
he had forgotten the sun.
And strange that when there was
that endless sense of falling,
he was glad of it.

Demeter

I'm summer's pride, the heart of the corn,
the swallow's sickle, the circle
of the not yet died
and of the unborn.

I'm summer's lease, the cash in the till,
the wet footprint in the shower,
the hour and then another hour
of the ignorable ill.

I'm summer's heart, the beat
of the drum in the barley straw,
the dressed-up festival, the masks, the bore,
the not worth living for.

I'm harvest, the olive trees,
crushed oil and seized grape,
the gift of life.
I promised only imperfection,
was almost everyone's wife.

Death Valley

'We heard of the bank vaults, the breakable acres,
the impossible strikes and charms,'
said the mouths as they sucked at the future.
But the sand-devils hissed back 'Harms'.

'Where are the fabulous gravels, the silvers,
the ores to braze into gold?'
cried the voices in the salt of the desert.
And the mountains echoed 'Old'.

'Where are wild horses, and endless whiskey,
and burros with panniers to fill?'
asked need through its stained bandannas.
And the burst stone whispered 'Ill'.

'Here's the dynamite. Here's the blue vein.
Here are the tracks of my friends,'
said the hand in his heyday to the water-jar
and the canyon's warning: 'Ends'.

'I've made the deposit, I've riddled the sunlight,
I've starved in the whore's deck of worth.
I've mined a hard million – but where am I going?'
And the dry river-bed coughed 'Earth'.

'Why is there blood on the edge of the shovel?
Why am I so alone?'
asked the end of the journey to the red rich rock.
And the pick-axe answered 'Own'.

'Is there anything left? Is anyone there?
Rare, rare as desert snow,
does the future come softly to save me and solve me?'
And the silence of Leadfield spoke. 'No.'

Song at Midnight

just why
>> the blackbird sings at midnight I
>> don't know

lamps glow
>> along the docks
>>> perhaps it's that

some quality of light
>> too early to be true
>>> comes clear as dawn

and still
>> the blackbird frets
>>> as if it's ill

blood in its throat
>> I use each note
>>> to cancel debts

mistakes
>> words waste and aches
>>> the days gone wrong

but for the song
>> I wouldn't work so late
>>> or wait

Migrants

I was the point of the poor
field of the famine year,
rash of the tuber's aim.
I was the hunch–back bride
and the kelp in the tide.
I've forgotten my name.

I was the face in the stone
whose voice was buried unborn
in the sail's hull.
I was the one who paid
the hunger you made.
I was the hill's skull.

I was the journey to come,
the weight in the empty room,
the navigable star.
I was the language you spoke
when your spirit broke
across America.

Bearings

From Bertraghboy all bearings take a line
       On Cashel mountain's mark
To clear Treh Island, Oghly, Croaghmore.
The summit happens as a kind of sign.
       Even in almost-dark
It's what a navigator's looking for,

Is where the compass can be fixed, and start
       To govern comings-in,
To keep keel sound up to a rope and quay.
A hull of hill has circumstanced the chart
       Through seaward discipline:
To take a bearing is a making free.

An Ashtray for San Francisco

The errant boys are falling into light
From memories of speed and Viet Nam.
Some opened restaurants. Some retain the right
To remain silent in their book of names
And shake all morning: 'What a fuck I am
To end up bumming dimes on Folsom Street.'
Some bought their Harleys just to hit the heat
Across the Golden Gate
As every gimcrack analyst declaims
'Where did the bad experiences start?'
A drug-store, midnight, and a broken heart.

Don't Walk. Don't spit don't ride don't smoke don't cough.
Remember how to grease. And park in line.
On 8th Street it's $5 to jack off
And mumblers to themselves replay the hurt
Whose accusations, daddy, made them shine
On vodka and a cup of coins. In bookstores
Full of laptops professorial bores
Chew nonsense in loose jaws
And windy graduates almost making out
Are theorists of the uselessness of art:
Cold coffee, midnight, and a broken heart.

You flew in from Vancouver, and were zoned,
Wild-eyed in Haight, the body-stocking ripped.
Marijuana. Over One Billion Stoned –
And looking for another dry embrace
To fend the fear that loneliness equipped
And wandered with in city streets all day.
'That bitching Rhonda. Thinks her shit is grace...'
Your $15 was too much to pay
To watch his come deface your resumé.
'He got his manners straight from AutoMart,'
A rat-faced midnight and a broken heart.

'A silly thing I have to figure out...'
'His Jaeger G-string... And she's doing dope,
Some tenement on 9th Street...' –
Messed up the rhythms as the childhood hope
Begins to bleed away
However far. 'And I can't hear her shout...'
Meanwhile the errant boys are falling, falling
Through all the hurt that was the last good lay,
And someone has forgotten that they're calling
A double-take – from LAX to JFK –
Whose tears are on the make, but scaled. And smart
The midnight, smart
The drug-store, smart
The crooked heart.

Presents

You pulled the new dress from its dollars
And thought about Christmas Day.
You tried on the dress for the mirror
That couldn't run away.
And what did the mirror reply, my dear?
That you were the fairest, the perfect, the brave?
A talented body that knew how to behave?
      O no, my dear, my love. That was sex,
      But what mirrors say is meant as a hex,
      And the mirror's reply
            Was I.

You took the new shoes from the shoe-box
And thought that they'd suit your career.
You arranged your hair in the toe-caps
As the leather started to leer.
Did the one who looked back leer or smile, my love?
Did it want a clear skin and an angled jaw?
Did it wonder what that briefest of frowns was for?
      O no, my fox, my coney, my dear.
      The gaze you found had already found fear
      And what fear must deny
            Is I.

You unwrapped the ring from its tissues
And thought about value and price.
You slipped it on your third finger
Then took it off. Twice.
And what was the ruby's reflection, my angel?
It had no chance to answer. It had seen your face
Taut with contempt, marked by disgrace.
      And yes, my dear. What the mirror had bred
      Was beauty, but what you'd seen instead
      Was what lies in the eye
            Of I.

Fishermen on Santa Monica Pier

Real life's defeated them across the world.
Wherever it may be –
from Santa Monica to the Red Sea –
they've always been old, always seen the waves
hush around the pier's end hurt as hope,
evolved a deepening shadow on the skin
and watched the sun go down, nothing to show
but the slow hours connected to a weight
where age is waiting, become
imaginary as the sun,
though it comes too late to riddle back,
to solve their going home again alone
with a mind full of photographs and bone;
ling, bass and huss; cut bait;
and that specific of the moon,
the lost ability to concentrate.

They spin their hands through shoals of pull and touch
to find simplicity, to wish the flood
come live, as if the act could prove
the past was tractable, made to behave
into a trick of eye and light, and now
the riding of a float hard by a stave...
They last real life, happen on all their ghosts
across the world whose country is Perhaps
and happiness, that lies much otherwise
than handbooks of the self assume,
and can't be gained by going, nor by maps.
But by connectedness and choice
of being where the end of age has happened
and is working out its furies in the deep
amendments of what brought it close,
they stand for silence and its gravities.

From the Country of Perhaps

It's always there, the country of Perhaps,
where it's an agreeable time to be betrayed
into the arms of a middle-aged cocktail waitress
and the warmth of a plausible high-rise bar
where the music is satisfyingly loud
and of no particular vintage
and no one knows or cares who you are —
or at least so you'd like to think
as you sip something quixotic
that's normally far too expensive to drink.

And of course it's a place where a public style
can usually be found for the private shames
of a face made ugly by repeating its sins
or not being able to finish the crossword.
There, too, the hesitant figures
who reel into the night and trip over hydrants
really can still play the movements of
complex sonatas and will see in the mirror
come morning a shape and gesture they can love.

At least the inhabitants have things in common:
all have been tempted to flee and have driven
at some cost down the eight-lane highways of guilt
where one-night hotels beckon them in
with neon arabesques and the offer
of complimentary *hors d'oeuvres*.
Their credit, like yours, is into the red.
They also hope for the ocean and look wistful
when easy deaths turn ugly, and photographs
of the dog-eared innocent are displayed with pride.

And all have made the valiant effort
at least for a moment to pursue
the moral imperatives of a changed life:
you can see how much it has taken,
how hard it is merely for them to be there,
confused by their passions, not knowing
how to use the cutlery or what to wear
or about tomorrow or whether to send,
post-marked from the country of Perhaps,
the letter that means less than they intend.

At Lindisfarne Priory

In the beginning
there were no *Safe Crossing Times*.
Remote the place,
endowed with stone and hope,
and tide ceaseless
as the activity of grace.

Succeeding names defined
access of a kind:
Aidan, Cuthbert, Chad –
whose words charmed
animals from the ocean,
weapons from woundings,
to the miraculous wood.

They understood
how prayer has to exist
as the voice of causeways and edges
and lives in windows where there's nothing
but coloured fragments of a day,
a hill growing out of a beach,
and the blue impossible sky
that's always but not quite
out of reach.

from *Mass*

Throw away the calendar,
The critical key.
Cancel the cleverness
That calls you free.

Discard the cheque-book,
The doubtful receipt.
All of your enterprise
Means your defeat.

Look back at history
As it pours into space
And into the mirror
Of your disgrace.

Run to the libraries,
Flock to the play.
Any diversion
Can please today.

The comfort of strangers,
The dubious sex,
Gorging on glances
A moment wrecks;

A theory of money,
The cash paradigm,
Leads to the precipice
Men made of time;

The forks and faces,
The glabrous paté…
You choke on the fish-bones
And sweat Chardonnay.

Stop conversation,
Ignore what you hear,
And still time's falling
From the edge of fear.

Resentment and ruin
Worry in the speech,
Intending conclusions
They can never reach.

Forget the scholarship.
Tear up the degree.
The success you paid for
Was temporary.

Temporary the culture,
Transient the friend,
Momentary the lovers
Love can't defend.

Efface the manuscript.
Send back the drink:
Fatuous alcohol;
Purposeless ink.

There's only forgetting,
There's memory's spoil.
But into the absence
Flow blood and oil.

I call it sacrament.
You call it waste.
But I eat Christ's body
With its bitter taste.

And there in the Eucharist
A seven-horned lamb,
The end of the sacrifice:
I am that I am.

from *Old English Poems and Riddles*
(2008)

The Seafarer

for Derek Britton

Truth? I can seal it   in song's reckoning,
tell its stories: times of hardship
I owned often,   unease and toil;
how I've borne both   bitterness and breast-care,
known sorrow's surges   in the surging keel,
wave-roiling terror –   they wore me, saw
the narrow night-watch   nailed to the boat-prow
as the cliffs unsteadied.   Cold, constriction:
my feet fettered,   frost-bound and cramped,
clamped, ice-locked, though   my cares ravened there,
hot round the heart,   and hunger tore
at the spirit's tiredness.   Time's slaves can't imagine –
those day-dawdlers   dwelling fair on land –
how I lived winter,   wretched, sorrowful,
on the exile's path,   an ice-cold sea,
deprived alike   of praise, friends, profit,
frost-candles in clothes,   flogged by hail-nails…
Nothing to hear there   but the hail, the sea-yell
on terror's frozen track.   At times, swan-voices
were diversion, a game,   or gannet's pluming –
whaup's weeping-song   instead of the world's laughter;
gulls' aimless cry   instead of the good mead-drink.
Tempests beat stone-cliffs,   and the tern answered,
ice-feathered one;   often eagle-kites
screamed, dew-feathered.   And yet scant or none
befriended my desolate   winter-faring.
Hard to believe it   for land-lubbers,
suburb-dwelling saps   with no sense alert,
for the wine-flushed, sottish,   but I was weary there,
having to last, to wait   on the lanes of sea.
Night-shower nipped,   and from the north, snow-squall;
rime-frost on earth-crust;   rife hail-stones' pelt,
each grain coldest.   And a cauldron of thought,
terror of imagining: *Onto such towering seas*
must I myself travel,   *onto the torn wave's holm?*

Yet I must, I must.   Moments compel me
to this due journey.   My duty's to seek
land out of longing,   land more lasting...
But there's no man on earth –   not with courage for manners;
not with goodness, nor gifts;   nor so gracious in youth;
nor so lavish in deed   or so loved by kings –
who isn't anxious   about what the ocean might claim,
what god guide him,   go where he will.
Harp-song's irrelevant,   as is ring-giving,
the pleasuring of women,   the promises of the world –
nothing matters more than   noise of the sea-roll,
dangerous longing   for doomed voyages.
Trees shake with blossom,   the towns grow fair
and meadows brighten,   the world quickens –
but the quickening warns   worry to its journey
drives the heart-thought   from its dithering
and onto the tide-races,   tracks of the ocean.
Still the cuckoo calls,   its cadence lament:
summer's guardian sings,   then sorrow's ordained,
bitterness, resentful.   Blessed is the citizen,
nestled in his nothings,   who knows nothing
of such vicious voyages,   nor ventures their limits.
Promise, compulsion   can't imprison a mind,
and mine is mettled   by the mere's slow flood,
ranges the whale-way,   the whole world's expanse,
the ocean's sheets –   and always returns
greedy, more eager   for going. Though the cuckoo
still yells of death   an irresistible Yes
urges me onward;   aches, God-given –
dearer and more dreadful   than a deadened life
of fidgets and flittings.   It's failure that warns
that nothing shall last   of the noise and wealth
of the world. And one   of these witnessing three
will always throw doubt   in the eyes of hours:
old age; sickness;   or the sword's envy –
each can bring judgement   at any just moment.
'Reputation,' then?   The ruck of the living
tells afterwards   of the talents of men,
who must earn opinion   before they end their span,
contending in time   with the tall hatreds,

opposing the devil   with purity of deed,
so that children to come   will have chance to praise
and their name number   among the new angels
always, always,   so that honour will last,
know bliss with the blessed.
                              Now blanked are the days,
all the opulence   of earth's kingdom:
no real rulers;   no royalty left,
nor gold-giving   granted as once there was.
Our ancestors shared   honour between them,
enjoyed justice,   were juried by fame…
But crumbled, declined   is that cache of dreams.
Now the world's witnessed   only by the weaker ones,
possessed by the hiss of sin.   Hand-shake's despised,
decency withers,   and decadence is rife
in the human souls   inhabiting the earth.
Age shall wither them   in turn. Ashen,
they'll mourn, grey-haired,   the merits of the past –
greatness, generosity   given back to time.
And when the flesh-home, the body,
                              starts to fail the spirit
they won't taste sweetness   but traffic in sorrow,
and – motionless – imagine   the might-have-been.
Brother buries brother,   buries gold in graves.
Clan and kinsman   are corpses, whose shrouds
sag with blood-money,   booty of conscience.
But to the soul that's sick,   whose sin chokes it,
money brings no merit,   no mercy from God,
however it's hoarded   in the here and now.
Great is God's power,   that girds even
                              the foundations of earth,
establishing forever   the strong earth's crust,
the land's fineness,   the firmament's roof.
Who won't dread his Redeemer
                              will die a fool – unprepared
                              for death's swiftness,
but who lives humbly   shall have his reward
                              from heaven's benison.
The Measurer's strength   ·shall install fortitude,
                              presence in the powerless.

Yet a man's self-control   must be trained, his mind
                made steadfast, resolute.
He should honour promises,   purity of manner.
It is moderation   that's the most of man –
faced with friend or foe,   a refined conscience.
Though foe will be fire,   conflagration,
so also the friend   whose fate's unwished.
But nevertheless   God's knowing is great,
his justice more just,   more genuine
                than any man's deeming.
Where, after all, is our home?   Our homecoming?
We should give our thanks,   thoughts to the journey,
and our long labour,   so that longing shall pass
to its appointed place,   praise the blessedness
whose life is vivid   in the love of God,
in heavenly hope.   To the Holy Lord, praise!
The Elder of Days   honoured and raised us,
Eternal Strength   stretched through eternity.
                Amen.

Deor

Women did for Wayland.   Inward with woe
the obsessed smith-god   suffered sorrow's all:
for travel companion   torment and longing,
winter's exile;   wretchedness was fated
after Nithhad's supple   sinew-brace had bound,
brutally, had condemned   the better of men.
       May this, may this   as that pass away.

The death of brothers?   To Beadohild it meant less,
was less grievous sore,   than her own self's trouble:
over-obvious,   easy to discover
she'd become pregnant.   In panic, she couldn't think,
simply decided   to settle for the worst.
       May this, may this   as that pass away?

We heard many could tell   of Meathhild's plight –
dreaming of water,   the wife of Geat
was sleep-deprived.   Sorrow made her love.
       May this, may this   as that pass away.

And Theodric?   For thirty years
too many knew how   he ruled Mearingburgh.
       May this, may this   as that pass away?

We entered the mind   of Ermanric's thought:
a world of wolves.   His wide empire
spanned Gothic peoples: grim sovereignty.
Many of the finest   lived fettered by sorrows,
expected only pain,   and prayed always
that such a kingdom   might be overcome.
       May this, may this   as that pass away.

Sorrow-care abides,   blanked of blessings,
dark-steeped in mind.   To a man's self it seems
that his dole of doom's   durable, endless.
And yet imagine: among the world
it's a witting God   grants change on change,

assurance to some,   to some graceful,
while to some, others,   he assigns sorrows.
And now something   of myself, my Self:
Once their harp-voice,   the Heodenings' song-maker,
I was loved by my lord –   dear loved, Deor named.
Many were the winters   I waxed in my song,
praised by patrons,   until Heorrenda – proud,
astute singer –   stole that estate
lords once lavished on,   once left to me.
          May this, may this   as that pass away?

A Riddle

My home's noisy.   I'm not. I'm mute
in this dwelling-place.   A deity shaped
our twinned journey.   I'm more turbulent than he,
at times stronger.   He's tougher – durable.
Sometimes I come to rest.   He always runs on ahead.
For as long as I shall live   I shall live in him.
If we undo ourselves,   death's due claims me.

Wulf and Eadwacer

It's as though a kind of gift   had been given to my people.
If he comes vicious,   it's him they'll want to capture.
We're differently placed.
On that island, Wulf;   I on this other.
Secure, that isle   caught among fenland.
Murder-minded,   men who inhabit it.
If he comes vicious   it's him they'll want to capture.
We are apart.
Over that wide distance   it's for Wulf I've longed.
Then it was rainy weather,   and I rigid, weeping
when his battledress   began to embrace me…
I took pleasure in it;   it was pain also.
Wulf – O my Wulf!   What wastes me now
is your absence,   infrequent visits,
lacklustre spirit,   not the lack of food.
D'you hear this, Eadwacer?   It's our wretched whelp
the wolf bears to the woods.
Easily sundered,   what wasn't ever of a piece:
our gift together.

The Wife's Lament

About my sorrowful self   this song I utter,
my self's turmoil.   I can tell truly
what of griefs I've gathered   since I grew up, both
new and old, but   never more than now.
Always I suffered   exile, misery,
and since my lord   left, left his kin,
went over the waves' expanse,   I've worried daybreak
with where, in which land   my lord might be.
    When I set out   to serve, join him –
friendless, governed only   by grievous need –
my man's kinsmen   met covertly,
secretly plotted   to separate us two
so that we'd live sundered,   go lonely in the world,
in the most wretched manner.   I was a mind, longing.
    My lord ordered me   to this ailing land.
I had no friends here   in this far country,
few dear or close.   Darkened is my thinking.
Then I thought I'd found   a fitting husband...
but one ill-starred,   aching in spirit,
withdrawn, whose plan   implied murder,
whose smile was a knife.   'Never,' we'd said, often,
'shall any violence   divide us – except death.
'And nothing else.' But   now that has changed,
now ripped away   as if it never had been,
our loving friendship,   and far or near
I'm forced to suffer   this feud of my Beloved.
    They forced me to live   in this forest clearing,
under the oak's branches,   in an earth-barrow.
Old, this earth-cave.   All I do's yearn.
Dark, these valleys   voided among hill-tops,
riddled with hedge-spikes   wrapped round with briars:
a joyless place.   Jealously, fiercely here
I think of my lord's absence.   There are lovers on earth,
those dear to, those disposed   in their dear one's bed,
while I, alone,   at first light will pace
around this ancient grave   under the oak's branches,
where I'm forced to sit   the summer-long day,

allowed to weep   longing, exile,
need's many hardships,   since I'm never able
to still, set at rest   the strife in my mind
nor the fraught longing   fetched me from life.
     The young always   should yearn to be serious,
     tough in character;   so too they should have
     good comportment,   whatever problems may press,
     what ravening cares.   Their right to be happy
     in the world's within…   There, far outcast,
it may be that my Dear One   – distant, stranded –
sits where storms hammer   at cliffs in hoar-frost,
lives weary in spirit,   by water marooned
in some desolate hall;   that my Dear Beloved
is mauled by sorrows,   remembering too often
a happier place.   But whosoever
lives in longing   shall alone find grief.

A Riddle

My dress? Darkness,   though each adornment's bright,
red-glittering, sheer: shining costume.
I misdirect   the reckless, guide a fool
on his fool's errand.   Others I stay from
necessary journeys.   No way of knowing
why they, maddened,   all thought stolen,
all acts aimless,   should amplify me –
waste, wrong-doing!   And they'll have woe for it
once Consequence comes,   unclasps its care-hoard,
if they haven't yet stopped,   are still obsessed.

The end of Beowulf (lines 3137–82)

The people of the Geats   then prepared for him
a fitting and proper   funeral barrow
hung with helmets,   hued with battle-shields,
with bright corselets,   just as he'd requested.
In its midst they laid   their mighty prince,
lamenting him, their beloved   lord and protector.
Grieving warriors   began to kindle
the pyre, built huge   on the high headland.
Smoke climbed and scattered   as swart wood caught
in a crackle of flame,   whose call mingled
with their tide of cries –   a tumult, dying
only when his body's core   broke, fire-eaten.
That death they grieved   with dirges, sorrow,
one death-lay sung   by a woman, who…
…   with hair bound up…
sang grief's concern,   whose song expressed
her fear that time   would fill with terror –
vicious invasion,   vile kidnap's killing,
humiliation…   Heaven swallowed the smoke.
Then those stricken people   constructed a place
on the headland's heel   – high-sheltered, broad,
visible to the horizon,   to those viking seas.
Ten days they built   this beacon, symbol
of their lord's courage.   Round what was left of ashes
they built a wall,   as well and splendidly
as their cleverest of men   could conceive it.
Into the mound they carried   the collars and jewels –
all the adornments   which envious hands
had once stolen   from the wondrous hoard.
They let earth hold those   ancient treasures,
left gold to the ground,   where again it rests,
useless, unprofitable,   as once before.
Twelve warriors rode   around the mound.
Known for bravery,   of noble descent,
they would claim and name   their numberless griefs,
utter in memory   an elegy for their king.
Stewardship they praised;   his strength and valour;

they mourned and assessed   his many virtues.
Fitting it is that   his fellows should praise
a man's memory   and merits with love
once his spirit's been fetched   from its frame of life.
And so they lamented,   these men of the Geats –
companions, a brotherhood –   the passing of their lord.
They said that of all   earthly rulers
he'd been the mildest man,   and the most gentle,
kindest to his clansmen   – and couth in fame.

The Ruin

A miracle, these walls,   though marred by time
were the shattered buildings,   shaken the giant-works.
The roofs are wrecked,   ruined are the towers,
plundered the bar-gate.   Plaster in frost-grip,
gables gaping –   collapsed, a gash
eaten out by age.   Earth's-grip has seized
masons, architects.   They're dismissed, perished
in hard ground's clutch.   Hundreds of generations
have passed since then,   while the place endured –
greying, red-stained   under gathering lichen –
in successive kingdoms,   sung at by storms.
Walls' curve declines...   ...crumbles still the...
...rent...penetrated...   ...
and grimly ground...   ...
...shone...   the...
...old monument,   ancient work...
...g...   bracelet, mud-encrusted.
Mind lit with promise, and swift-purposed,
could build a curve,   bound the determined
foundations together   by dint of iron.
Then bright were the rooms,   the bath-houses,
multiply-gabled,   man-noise within,
halls full of mead   and human pleasures –
till terror, that is time,   took all away.
Plague, slaughter came,   days of pestilence.
The viciousness of death   touched valiant men.
Their bastions withered   into waste places,
their city decayed,   its kindlers perished,
its armies became dust.   Desolate, therefore, these strongholds,
whose red-curved roof   is ravaged, its tiles
a garrison of decline.   It's merely ruined ground,
a pile of rubble.   Promising fighting-men,
glad, gold-adorned,   glittering in armour,
preening in wine-flush,   moved proud, once, in trappings.
It was treasure they saw –   silver, gem-stones,
riches, power,   wrought stones of earth,
the airy breadth   of a beautiful city.

Stone houses stood;   stream cast a current,
a whelm of heat,   where a wall compassed
its bright ambit.   Baths were placed there,
a central warmth,   snug, convenient.
From there a gout of...   ...
over the grey stone-work,   gushed warm currents
und...   ...
in circular pools.   The pouring streams
...   into the bathing-place.
Whenever...   ...
...   it's a royal custom,
how the...   ...city...

from *Polder*
(2009)

Polder

It was born from waving, from sand islands
disappearing into mist, from the goodbyes
to the ships with their freight of expensive religion
vanishing towards the Baltic, a fret of masts
like rigged needles disappearing into the sea.

How, then, to maintain, how sustain
water-tight Holland, guilty but ingenious,
against the nails of the north wind
and the narrows of the night-watch
or inundations of the day?

This is the answer beyond farewell, Godspeed –
more about puddings than metaphysics:
Protestant pumping-stations, the low machinery
turning fathom to mulch, mulch to pasture…
Not scenery, but reclamation.

And yet it dreams of waves.
A ship was its ambition.

The Thorn Carol

I tried to get home, but couldn't find the place:
Fell-side, caul-water; trees filled with grace;
A string of cold blossom; ironwork below
The green-stained barb of the hawthorn-O.

I searched along footsteps from years before.
They led to someone else's door.
I asked for directions. There was nowhere to go
But the green-stained barb of the hawthorn-O.

I tracked down the map of myself for a key
To the lock that was missing. What was missing was me.
I yelled for remission, in the air and snow.
The reply was the barb of the hawthorn-O.

I went through nine cities, through the knocking shops,
To the end of the bottle when the music stops,
Looked in the letters and the rain's brilliant bow
For the green-stained barb of the hawthorn-O.

Lately a scholar, whose cavil was called hearse,
Lately a book in its powers… They curse
The distance of lamp-light whose edges grow
The green-stained barb of the hawthorn-O.

I want to get home but I don't know where.
The taxi-driver set fire to my hair.
The trains ran down darkness, the rivers didn't flow
Past the green-stained barb of the hawthorn-O.

I hungered through winter, had winter's voice.
I shouldn't have come back here but I had no choice:
The starving rain-drop; the bricks fed with snow;
And the green-stained barb of the hawthorn-O.

Murdering the Sea

to a child

Why there are windmills is because
they fought the sea, the *rijk*
of herring-gull, the whale's-way,
the slow struggle of the anemone –

lifted it in sail-cloth arms
throttled for sky, and ate the wave
till here where you are could burn,
and the ploughshare come dry.

As far as you look is artifice
or put to work: the air
fills oyster-shells with snow; you're borne
by weeks of earth and ice; and deep
under the Amsteldijk carp sleep.

An Auction for Amsterdam

That man, who recently acquired –
     for an astronomical price –
     the old Dutch master,
I wish him well, I wish him well.
It turns out that this hitherto-neglected, until-now-
     unattributed piece of transcendent
     Biblical hokum
wasn't anyone's to sell.

Imagine avarice, locked in
     its 22nd floor office with its Dic-
     taphone and its cruel secretary,
its bank of screens, its plasm of phones.
Hands crook round the Eagle atop the walking-frame,
     but nothing moves except the brightening eyes
     that get their promises to keen
among a nest of deals and bones.

And what's he bought, that man? A prophet
     in a 17th century, Thank-God-I've-made-it pose:
     I travelled, then studied Greek; then put that by for guilders.
Now here I am. Now here I am.
Nonesuch, I sit and watch them every day. They move in
     rimless glasses, architects of coffee, raincoats, air,
     on any street that crawls the smell of drains
in Amsterdam, in Amsterdam.

To the last most intricate detail, they too
     have wives wear sharpened scissors, dirty toenails;
     down to the valves and palp, breasts and bush consumed:
mute need; burnt night. And then the night
whose ochre grumbles as it pays, or scratches
     stub-ends of its brush. The technicalities of skin admire,
     geometry of moon betray –
and bleed them white, and bleed them white.

And what the eyes just paid for is this
    culture that means everywhere, yet is no one's –
    a finicking insistence on the peripheral, pathetic,
                    over-obvious bowl
of withered flowers; the starveling dog.
These things are home, they nag between the tapestries,
    dust falls and lies, whatever light. While outside... Outside...
    Perhaps he knows, the man who rooked the master. If so,
he bought the fog. He bought the fog.

The February Fences

When there's a big wind from the south-west
the garden
      tilts. February
is moss and rain and non-alignment.

The fences, for example, all February
lean from the south-west,
inch by inch distorting the garden.
You can't put them back into alignment

however much you faff about in the garden
with plugs and hammers. It's February,
Atlantic weather and the south-west,
lattices and uprights out of alignment.

The discipline is the snowdrops at the back of the garden.
They know nothing of alignment or even February,
or how its fences encroach on the garden from the south-west.

They hang frail hoods against the weather.
It's not even a question of learning what to do.
It's because of the leaning rain, the non-alignment.
They have no angles. Therefore they are true.

Fado

During the raid, the fado
escaped from the brothel, crawled

along the docks: blood
flowering into rain-water; a shred of leather

on the edge of a diamond; rose petals
from the bedside bowl disfiguring

the surface of poison in a glass;
future of midnight a rosary of sirens.

A moment of emotion is the structure
of a cry with blood in its throat.

By dawn the local tragedy's locked up
but its meaning is still at large –

a girl wiping off her make-up; bruises as icons
whose names are becoming songs

repeating, repeating, changing
and remembering until all

the urban disasters have the purpose
of saints, the windows are unbroken,

and the terrible facsimiles of failure and love
have become love.

The Gravy People

Cheap cuts of meat after the war – tripe and lights
And eking out. Making do. It was almost a style.
And we were gravy people.
Without the gravy nothing was a meal.

And eking out? Making do, that was the style:
Half a pound of butter and a sewing kit.
But without gravy nothing was a meal.
After a while you made the best of it.

Half a pound of butter and a sewing kit.
You'd never think we'd won a war.
After a while you made the best of it.
There was so much you just learned to ignore.

You'd never think we'd won the war.
For years we queued for stamps to feed the ration book.
There was so much you just learned to ignore.
If you complained you got a funny look.

For years we kept those stamps up in the ration book.
The best was cod and chips.
No one complained. You'd get a funny look.
There were no pretty clothes. And as for foreign trips…

The best was once a month, those cod and chips.
Apart from that… Cigarettes, and lard.
You wanted pretty clothes, or sea-side trips,
But soon forgot them, and it wasn't hard.

We won the war on tea and cigarettes and lard,
On patience, mending, knowing not to feel.

And lights, or tripe? They make a lovely meal.
It wasn't hard. We were gravy people.

for clive	/s/	cott
	s	katers
in all thi	s	
	s	lither
one	θ	ink
	s	of
wordswor	θ	
being pur	s	ued by
manias in the	f	orm of mountains
('we hi	s	ed along the
poli	ʃ	ed
/aɪ	s/	' etc.)
	h	ere in the
colde	s	t march
	f	or
	θ	irty years
	h	olland
	ʃ	arpens
it	s	blades
crouches over the	s	pine of a
	s	kate
but thi	s	year the *el*
	f	
	s	*tedentocht* is
	s	ta
	ʃ	ionary
though all the polders ru	ʃ	to the
nor	θ	
we	s	t
in the direction of gra	s	mere,
fa	s	
	/t/	

Witness

Undo the rope from the rafter, young lover,
Give the sunlight back its crutch.
Prise the note from its crack in the mortar
Old fingers can't touch.

Now take me down to the river, young lover,
And chill my lips with chalk.
Unclothe me, wash me in the cool water,
Then teach me to talk.

Sit me under the willow, young lover,
Where the leaves in the wind turn white.
Don't stay to listen. Head back to the slaughter
With your eyes full of spite.

You'll disappear for good, young lover,
No syllable prove you'd been there.
Time is the hands of the hangman's daughter,
And I am air.

Ithaka

He asked for a passage to Ithaka
at the wrong season of the year.
With all its magnetism leased
the compass was neither West nor East.
There's no Ithaka, insisted the needle North.
No Ithaka, mumbled the reluctant South,
No Ithaka here.

He asked for the way to Ithaka
from the city drunks and the winter snows.
It'll cost, sighed the traffic to a passer-by.
It'll cost, choked the bottle, and began to cry.
It'll cost, said the petals of a steel flower
to the credit card, that had just bought an hour
with a Christmas rose.

He invented a route to Ithaka
out of a trinket he found in the street.
A shop-window mannequin mopped its brow
with a hamburger wrapper stained with here and now.
You won't go far on that, my dear —
just as long as it takes you won't take a year.
And think of the heat.

He looked on the ring-road for Ithaka
but the signposts had strayed, or turned into thorn,
and the only maps were fragments of prayer.
Our Father, said the ages of anywhere.
Our Father, said the riddle of the lover's letter.
Our Father, said the zenith, *but it would have been better*
if you'd never been born.

He consulted the grammars for Ithaka.
That is my country, he thought, *with its long*
declensions, its morphology of time,
its optative mood and its poems that don't rhyme.
That is my country, and I'll make it exist.
But an older voice began to insist
that the grammars were wrong.

He bought all the guidebooks to Ithaka,
but the relevant pages had been torn away.
People always do that, said the bookseller's smile.
You could call the Helpline. But the telephone dial
connected him with a harassed priest
who knew nothing of Ithaka. *Not in the least.*
Where *did you say?*

He indexed the small ads for Ithaka,
found no one who went by the name.
Two Roxanne's, an Amanda, and a private address
promised magical journeys, but nevertheless
they were bored by Ithaka. *Isn't it Greek?*
Hey, lover, same time, same place next week.
Glad that you came.

Time happened, as he looked for Ithaka –
into the different gardens thirty years of hail
fell and melted; the decades of birdsong
strewed the Zodiac, migrating among
its annual amendment; green came and went.
No point blaming time, time's innocent.
But nor is it frail.

Four consecutive passports for Ithaka.
He squinted from photographs, each of them bad.
On the first a young man trying to look old.
On the second a teller who wouldn't be told.
On the third the worrier, whose symptoms were cash.
And the fourth's stare narrowed through stubble and ash
at what Ithaka had:

Ithaka paid for the gate and the ticket
whose music was paper and comb.
It sponsored the needle, found the needle erratic,
the anaesthetist watching a mess of static;
the inhaler at the bedside; the gardens frozen.
And only Ithaka to grieve for the life it had chosen
that couldn't be home.

The Mill

Jacob Maris, *De afgesneden molen*, 1872. Rijksmuseum, Amsterdam

Elsewhere is ochre, sombre
this crust of ice, your breath.

It's how the wind's cut:
horizontal. You're narrowing your eyes.

Your journey's been scraped
from monochrome. You've been flensed.

Already you're grudging the cold –
brambles stiff in the ginnel,

that smear of frost.
Darkness in daylight.

There's no one else on the road.
It's happening to you.

You're grease, surviving
these stricken provinces.

And shortly nightfall.
Nowhere left to go.

Woman Reading a Letter in Blue

Vermeer, *Brieflezende vrouw in het blauw*, 1663–4.
Rijksmuseum, Amsterdam

It's how in moments of crisis
you notice
the blue nape of the chairs,
the highly polished buttons
stitching the upholstery,
and completing one wall
the polders in tapestry.

And here she is, in the vertical
spaces of now, the debris
of a well-kept house –
so engrossed in the letter
she holds it in two hands.
One leaf's already through,
discarded. Elsewhere
light's collecting
on a string of pearls,
high-angled and blue.

Neither smiling nor unsmiling
she'll read this letter forever.

A moment sooner, and she would have been
too quickly taking off her coat.
A moment later, and she would have been
leaning on the table for support.

But it will always be now.
That child will never be born.

Old Woman Reading

Rembrandt van Rijn, *An old woman reading* (*Lezende oude vrouw*),
1631. Rijksmuseum, Amsterdam

The painting is thought by some critics to be a representation
of the prophet, Anna. Others think it is a representation of
his mother, Neeltgen (Nellie).

I told that child
he mustn't flatter. *All that matters
is the Book*, I said, *God knows*.

That headscarf
was braid of Leyden best, and gold-embossed.
The detail had to take him hours,

working the light thick
until it made a head and book that weighed
a dam of shadows. Still my right hand froze.

Some kind of rapt
arthritic gold. Inauthentic. Old.
The saints I read don't really look like that.

Besides, you can't make out
the words I had to touch. The Book's not even Dutch.
From what I saw, I only seem at ease.

He never tells me
what he makes. For all the prophets he can fake
I wish he'd do a Proper Job.

The Storm

Ludolf Bakhuyzen, *Ships in distress in heavy storm*, c. 1690.
Rijksmuseum, Amsterdam

The concluding quote was lifted directly from the commentary
on Bakhuyzen's painting as this was found in the 2004
exhibition *The Masterpieces.*

However you see a blowsy seascape
he was trying for the epic
as a question of urgency
and how to do those waves.

That the North Sea has no dignity
and isn't Dutch? It is dirty and immortal.
It smashes ships as matters of technique.
Its surface trade is relics on the Scheldt.

Those waves aren't Protestant.
The drowning cries are what you get
for your money in this world, madam.
Of course our ambitions are matchwood.

You have never seen a painting
whose over-obvious waves so anxiously ask
*How mortal am I? Do you admire
how true to life I've been?
What will they say of me?*

They will say that *It is said
that in bad weather Bakhuyzen
often went out to sea.*

Horace in the Sabine Hills

In this loneliness
I've noticed an inclination to address fragments of poems
To the plants in the garden, which thrive on the lyric gift
In this loneliness
And a tendency to harrumph, to mock, or to repine
At the dismantling of the things, places and people
Who used to make life bearable, and even fair
In this loneliness
Hanging around in a dirty old habit,
Lusting after the ladies who bring me the news,
Finding everything harder to finish,
And forgetting – though forgetting is also a mercy
In this loneliness
I'll probably end up admiring exotic trees
Or banging on about Empire, while at the back of my head
There's a little refrain of interest to no one except the unfinished
                                                                    poem
Whose nature is both incremental and exhausting.
Well, one has done one's best
In this loneliness
Perhaps I should advertise. The problem there is
One finds oneself becoming over-ordered, and I should imagine
That difficult to live with. And besides, I tried –
Only to find the structure deficient in those quantities
I managed with ease in the old days, and the hand
Always, and always unbidden, writing out the phrase
In this loneliness

A Letter to Torquatus

Frankly I don't know how you can stand it —
For months the same broken doors in the kitchen;
The relics of weeks-old meals on the bedspread;
Vitreous stains that haven't received due attention.
But perhaps after all a life should be measured
By the capacity for bearing what its critics call squalor,
And equally, perhaps it's merely over-fussy
Or prurient to find dirt somehow deficient,
Whereas clearly it's a symptom of long-drawn-out resentment
That begins in the classroom, ramifies through families,
Dispatches its lovers late at night to the wine-shops
And will drop its fag-ash even into the open palm
That has begun to beckon towards the final judgement.

You might take it, Torquatus, as a species of sympathy —
Though you'll see only nit-picking antiquity
And tell me robustly to mind my own business.
Quite right. A man so lonely
That for company he murmurs at saplings
Or drones over-loudly about the dubious merits
Of olive oil or sea-bathing
Has no right to engage with the intricate choices
Of others. Still… How many decades, between us?
Truth is I've admired your insouciance
In the face of time and non-being,
And the years have allowed me, down to dust and atoms,
To compose the lineaments of order, called friendship.

I will look for your smile even as my monologue
Makes the women fall asleep in their soup-plates.
You will look for my approval among a chaos of nurses.
We shall slip into the dark out of step, but hand in hand.

Ochre

Striving, Torquatus:
the incessant hiss
of endless busy-ness.
You seem to simmer

in a world of scrolls,
anxious among patrons,
steaming at each hint
of distance or dislike –

a heat–haze
disfiguring the great
while the crowd's every commonplace
gesture trembles.

Here it's full summer,
so much dust in the sky
that the burnt moon rises
in all its ochres...

...She is the last of my loves,
patient, imperious.
I am slowly unburdened
where her appraisal dances –

old enough to know
that to get where you want to go
then it's usually necessary
to begin somewhere else.

Roads

Let us have no religions, Torquatus, except those which belong
To roads and libraries, to a code of manners whose primary purpose
Is the maintenance of parks and fountains. In such belonging,
Whose polity is the most artful avoidance of shame,
At least one's loneliness can be stroked by civic duty
While being soothed by old architectures in public gardens.
No need, in that context, to invent a wood,
Sacred or otherwise, where some shit-smeared seeress
Rants tearfully about the magic properties of acorns
Or the glass-spindled blood-sword that will choose the slain
And fetch them to the messy and exhaustive deflowering
Of virgin rivers, where ululation is unfortunately compulsory.
Such enthusiasm leads merely to nothing to read:
Their runes of grief are all very well, but such
Over-simplicity, one finds, is the better confronted
If there's a definite place in which to dawdle, or better yet,
A comfortable spot at which to sit down.

By the Germans' keenness for meaning discovered
In the bowels of sacrifice I'm left disconcerted.
What to make of the Semnones, whose pubic hairs
Are hallowed by auguries? The Idisi, whose horses' entrails
Unbind any fetters? The Chatti, who ritually deflesh
Their priests and pour libations through a skull's colander
In order to secure from the crudities of the heavens
Not, as one might expect, a bountiful crop of asparagus
But an assurance that their enemies shall soon be visited
By a plague of – of all things – frogs? Such fundamentalism
Can't, naturally it can't, endure teasing, and is therefore
A fit subject only for gawps or the circus.
Yet are we, Torquatus, havering among scrolls,
So very different? I suppose we are. It's why I write
Of roads and libraries, since it's only on the civilised journey
That one can cultivate any sense of the erotic, and only
Among books that posterities can in their ruin share
Their spoiled democracy of post-coital sadness.

Still, and finally, we're distinguished from the barbarian
By the fact that their depressions are so dismally local:
A circle of beech-leaves; a resentful mere
Whose brood is monstrous; a pitiful altar
Insisting that its broken stones are somehow animate;
Brittle braids of hair adapted as amulets
To appease the fingers of drowned girls in river-pools…
Our Mercury, at least, implies that distances exist,
That trade must travel, that engineers, cartographers
Never need be unemployed. Besides which, of course,
Any theory of maps must involve the exploitation
Of edges – not the sulks of the oracle, but strategy,
Whose pointer, scratching at the calm of the library, obliterates
Exclusively, and after due reflection. It's there, in that tactical
Pause, that she must slowly disrobe, there
Slave watch incuriously while skin is bitten in the name
Of pleasure, there good alliance determine the future –
Whose roads make our verses, our measured syllables
Which else couldn't be told from indiscriminate sobbing.

The Vinegar Days

for Grevel Lindop

Do you too wince, Torquatus – and if so, with aversion
Or reluctant affection? – as you remember the days
Left standing in vinegar, the vinegar days?
Hours of failed strategy, the foreplay to… to what?
The seduction from which one woke with a start
Having drooled on her shirt?
After the diplomatic handshake, turning away
From one's over-suave host into the evening
And then on the serenely raked path smiling
(One hopes with indulgence) at the climacteric
Of frotting groans and squeaks spawned
From the dark back of barbed wire at the yard's end
Where someone was had, and the other done?
Nights when the vine was the imaginary friend
One clutched for support in the taxi home
As one wept – how one wept! – for Rome?

They were vinegar days, and those supple,
Those abstemious, those cunning, less literal –
Those riddling their remaining senatorial lock
Too carefully across their crowns, those speaking
For effect in unfamiliar accents, the declamatory fools –
They warned us, or didn't warn us,
And have taken our places.
Of those gentle, those unconvinced – the best are gone
With the work unfinished, translated
Into a place where neither you nor I can pose.
The taxis no longer ply down the line of lights.
Sombre-eyed, fussy, still occasionally somewhere wheeled on
Like some unholy relic to cant something almost sensible,
I glance at fifty – abrupt, beaten, indefensible.

And here, in the flat, assumptive province
Called exile it's been autumn since winter. Although
The volumes have been alphabetised and a fire lit,
For months the house has been tossed in dry northerlies,
Familiar plants are early stripped, and the damaged leaf
Is burned with last year's paperwork to scurf.
No one told me that I'd have to learn
Such competence with grief.
I stare out, walk, take random routes, remembering
How happy... How hopeless... *The vinegar days.*
Only to my dearest friends, I write —
Usually to find them partly dismantled or wholly gone away —
While the white wind raves across the whitening clay.

Index of Titles and First Lines

Titles are set in italic, ignoring definite and indefinite articles.